IMAGES
of America

EFFINGHAM COUNTY

On the cover: Henry H. Dust, far left, operated a tire store at 111 West Jefferson Street in the 1920s. Pictured in this 1927 shot are Dust, his dog Ted, employee Ed Stumborg, daughter Agnes, and Eugene Greuel (as the Michelin Man). Agnes, who later married Ed Althoff, worked 31 years for the Illinois State Police and ended her long life as sole proprietor of the Cloverleaf Motel, which she operated until her death on February 3, 2008, at age 99. (Courtesy of Agnes Dust Althoff.)

IMAGES
of America

EFFINGHAM COUNTY

Kate Keller Bourland and Bill Grimes

ARCADIA
PUBLISHING

Published by Arcadia Publishing
Charleston, South Carolina

Library of Congress Catalog Card Number: 2008936745

For all general information contact Arcadia Publishing at:
Telephone 843-853-2070
Fax 843-853-0044
E-mail sales@arcadiapublishing.com
For customer service and orders:
Toll-Free 1-888-313-2665

Visit us on the Internet at www.arcadiapublishing.com

To all the past, present, and future citizens of the county of Effingham.

CONTENTS

ACKNOWLEDGMENTS

This book would not have been possible without the generous gifts of images and conversation by many people. We have decided to show who gave us photographs and who provided us with caption information. We apologize if we have omitted anyone.

In chapter 1, "Transportation," photographs were provided by Rosemary Smith Percival, John Sills, and Fred Katz. Information was provided by Bruce Kessler and Charlie Slavens.

In chapter 2, "Effingham City," photographs were provided by Mary Ellen Eversman and Nora Niccum. Information was provided by LoElla Baker, Eleanor Bounds, Audrey Garbe, and Bill Broom.

In chapter 3, "Effingham Business," photographs were provided by Agnes Dust Althoff, Frank Stewart, C. F. Keller, Phyllis Sur Utz, John Kirby, Maxine Jaycox Gravenhorst, and Isabel Lustig. Information was provided by Maxine Jaycox Gravenhorst, Candy Jaycox, Greg Koester, Jack Thies, and Hank Stephens.

In chapter 4, "Schools and Churches," photographs were provided by Kay Althoff Adams, Frank Stewart, and Norma Bushue Verdeyen. Information was provided by Pastor Paul Bauer, Pastor Ed Roman, Laura Knierim, Rev. Gehl Devore, and Kay Althoff Adams.

In chapter 5, "Teutopolis," photographs were provided by Adeline Barclay, Tony Weber, and Patty Lidy Pruemer. Information was provided by Jim Burford, Rick Siemer, John Wessel, Bob Wernsing, Kurt Weber, Mack Kitten, and Tony Weber.

In chapter 6, "Altamont/Beecher City," photographs were provided by Pat Hogge Smith and Steve Miller. Information was provided by Pat Hogge Smith, Norm Miller, Steve Miller, Bill Wendling, and Bruce Kessler.

In chapter 7, "Other Places," photographs were provided by Ann Schultz Deters, Jim Schultz, and Melba Rice Henderson. Information was provided by Bob Schultz, Jane Schultz Herman, June Bushue, Rachel Boone, Barb Gillam, Bill Baxter, Regina Baxter, Doris McKinney, Milton McKinney, Lisa Flach Jewell, Melba Rice Henderson, and Jack Keller.

In chapter 8, "The Brothers Fitch," the photographs were provided by Chris Huff.

INTRODUCTION

However one describes Effingham County, the defining thread of its history is transportation. First there was the National Road—America's first national highway. Pres. Thomas Jefferson authorized construction of the road in 1806. Construction began in 1811, and crews reached Effingham County by 1829.

Some white settlers were already here by the time the National Road was built. Griffin Tipsword is typically credited with being the first white man to settle in what is now Effingham County in 1815. Tipsword, and those who came after him, has been the minority. The vast majorities who have passed through Effingham County over the years have kept going. Still, enough have stayed so that the county has a current population of about 35,000. People started staying in significant numbers after the National Road was completed. There was quality farmland and—for the most part—a moderate climate.

Effingham County was formed in 1831, 13 years after Illinois gained statehood. The first county seat was Ewington, a settlement on the Little Wabash River about three miles west of the current city of Effingham. Ewington thrived to a point, but its days as a major town were numbered in 1856 when the Illinois Central Railroad bypassed the town on what would become a Chicago to New Orleans route. That was good news for the tiny town of Broughton.

After county voters opted to move the county seat to Broughton in 1860, the town's name was changed to Effingham. With the Illinois Central Railroad running north–south and the St. Louis, Vandalia and Terre Haute Railroad running east–west, Effingham became a thriving railroad town in the last quarter of the 19th century.

Railroads were king in the late 19th and early 20th centuries, but the increasing popularity of the automobile caused the public to clamor for improved "hard roads." The people were obliged with two such national highways in the 1920s, now known as U.S. Routes 40 and 45. Effingham maintained its status as a national crossroads as a result of these two roads.

That crossroads status has remained the same in modern times. After Pres. Dwight Eisenhower signed the Interstate Highway Act in 1956, the limited-access highways were built in every state of the union, including Illinois. Effingham became the junction of Interstates 57 and 70, which remains the case today. One can stand at an interstate overpass and count license plates, or more easily, visit a business establishment near the interstates to see people from not only the United States but also many foreign countries.

As previously mentioned, Effingham has also been a final destination for many thousands of folk over the years. Perhaps the most dramatic ethnic migration over the years was that of the Germans. Catholic Germans first settled in the Teutopolis area in 1839. Later on, German Lutherans settled the Altamont area.

We have tried to capture a small part of our county's rich history through photographs, both of town and country, home and business, church and school. We hope we provide a suitable snapshot of what Effingham County has been all about for more than 175 years.

One

TRANSPORTATION

The diamond was where the Illinois Central Railroad (IC) and Pennsylvania Railroad tracks met. In this photograph, a westbound Pennsy train is passing the depot sometime in the 1950s. The IC line has since been reduced to one track.

Here is the St. Louis Limited swinging through the Teutopolis depot before the age of diesel. The St. Louis, Vandalia and Terre Haute Railroad came to Teutopolis around 1870. This railroad merged with the Indianapolis and Terre Haute Railroad to become the Vandalia Railroad in 1905. The Vandalia line merged with the Pittsburgh, Cincinnati, Chicago and St. Louis Railroad in 1917. The Pennsylvania Railroad leased the line in 1921 and ran it until 1968. The line is now operated by CSX of Jacksonville, Florida.

This is a Pennsylvania Railroad work/sleeping car, as it looked on May 3, 1959. The vertical-wood-sided car was built in 1907 and was yellow with black lettering. East–west passenger travel through Effingham County ended in 1968.

This image brings lyrics to mind: "I hear the train a-coming / Rollin' round the bend." A lone bystander sits on the fence alongside Lake Kanagga as a westbound Vandalia passenger train rumbles through during the early 20th century.

A westbound St. Louis, Vandalia and Terre Haute Railroad passenger train is crossing the old Salt Creek bridge between Effingham and Teutopolis in 1892. This bridge had 65-foot pilings that were replaced when the new bridge was built.

Before diesel, trains ran on coal and coal chutes, such as this one, served as fueling stations. This Pennsylvania Railroad *American* train is coaling up south of the current Effingham High School football field and U.S. Route 40.

Coal chutes and water towers were found along many railroad lines throughout the United States and anywhere else there was a rail line. This chute near Effingham was still under construction on December 2, 1916.

The Wabash Railroad depot was located on West Fayette Avenue on what was then the edge of town. The depot was later moved downtown, where it is still used as an insurance office.

Not only was Effingham a crossroads, but the city was also a shipment point, particularly for agricultural goods. In this photograph, livestock is being loaded onto a Pennsylvania Railroad train for shipment in the southwest corner of Effingham around 1940.

Railroad cars and engines were maintained in roundhouses, so named because many of them were circular in shape. By November 7, 1917, when this photograph was taken, even rectangular maintenance buildings, such as this IC shop south of the Effingham diamond, were called roundhouses.

Coal chutes were fixtures along railroad tracks until the 1950s, when railroads switched to diesel engines. This chute was located on the IC tracks near Effingham. The photograph was taken on March 15, 1912.

Here is another shot of the diamond in the late 1940s, before the new water tower was built behind the depot. The old standpipe that previously stored water for the community stands above the trees in the upper left of the photograph.

The Effingham Garden Club created this enduring symbol of Effingham, between the union station and the diamond. This heart-shaped plot, planted with flowers in season, is the first thing passengers would see in the depot area. Railroad employee George Katz took this photograph in 1950 from the second floor of the switching tower, known to railroad men as the FE tower for the telegraph call sign.

Not only did steam engines need coal, but they needed water too. In settled areas, outlets such as this one on the IC tracks provided water. The IC freight house is to the right, while the old city standpipe is in the upper left.

Sometimes disaster struck on the railroad, such as this head-on collision on September 6, 1916, between two freight trains on the IC spur southeast of Effingham, resulting in the death of one employee. The line was a spur line that enabled trains to run through Dieterich; Linton, Indiana; and Indianapolis.

Every little town had its own railroad stop in the early years of the 20th century. In the second decade of the 20th century, these people are waiting for the train at Dexter, a small town between Effingham and Altamont.

Here on May 16, 1922, workers are taking a break from building a bridge over the Little Wabash River for the road that would later be designated U.S. Route 40.

This group installed signals in an IC elevated line through downtown Chicago, as well as all signals for the electric division of the IC in the mid-1920s. The foreman was the shorter man on the far left of the front row, Hubert Keller. As H. G. Keller, he became better known as the owner of Keller Furniture in Effingham.

18

Firemen tended the coal-based fires that made railroads run in the steam era. It was hot, dirty work, but these guys occasionally got the chance to clean up and go out for special occasions. This group of Vandalia Railroad firemen around 1900 includes, from left to right, (first row) Harve Brunk, Jack Schmidt, Jim Hood, Billy Crise, Dan Crise, and Tom White; (second row) Les Wood, Mart Jones, Jim Lett, Bill Blakesly, Bob Craig, B. Hale, George Mitbeck, and Roy Purce.

Here is the north abutment of what would become U.S. Route 45 over Little Salt Creek southeast of Watson on June 10, 1921. Many locals still believe that a more appropriate name for Little Salt Creek would be "Bugs Creek," because of the abundance of insects in the area.

Here is a crew working on what would become U.S. Route 40, east of Altamont. The men to the right are washing mortar off recently laid brick. The highway would eventually be overlaid with asphalt.

Women and children enjoyed watching the men lay brick for U.S. Route 40 near Altamont. State Route 11, later known as U.S. Route 40 after being federalized in the late 1920s, curved over the Pennsylvania Railroad tracks west of Effingham. The authors' guess is that this photograph was taken on a warm day sometime in the mid-1920s.

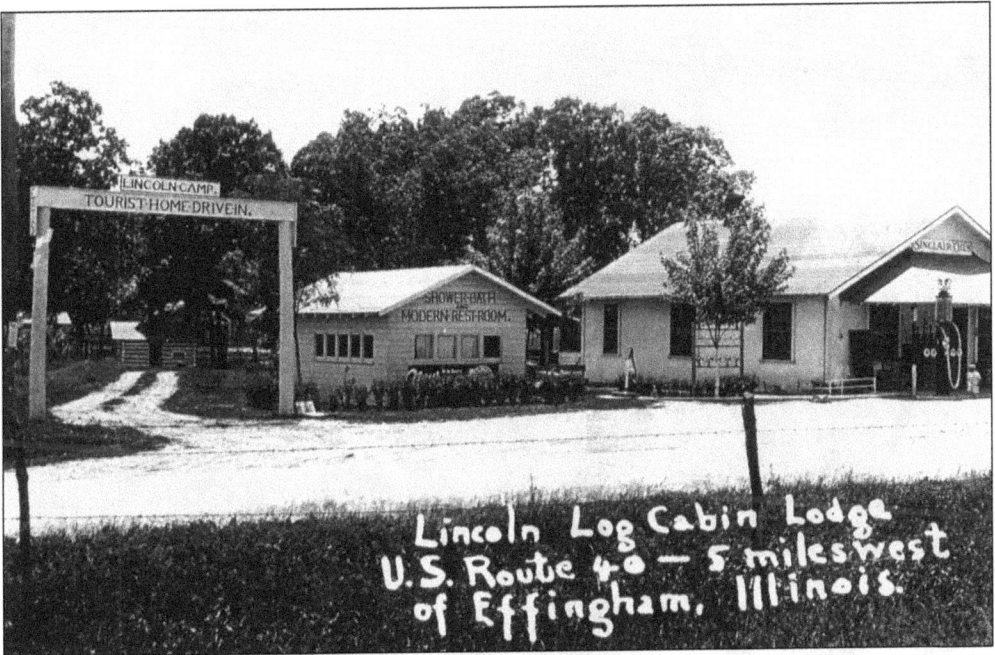

Lincoln Log Cabin Lodge
U.S. Route 40 — 5 miles west
of Effingham, Illinois.

As the federal highway system became more established and more people owned cars, an entire genre of businesses grew up along the highways, including gas stations, restaurants, and lodging facilities, such as this Lincoln Log Cabin Lodge located about halfway between Effingham and Altamont. Just as is the case today, businesses used amenities to compete with one another. At the Lincoln Log Cabin Lodge, amenities included showers and a modern restroom (probably with indoor plumbing). The filling station sold Sinclair gasoline.

Greyhound bus lines have had a long presence in Effingham. In the 1930s, when this photograph was taken, the bus stopped in front of the Raleigh Hotel on Banker Street next to city hall. Eventually a new depot, including the Post House restaurant, was built on Fayette Avenue to serve bus customers. Greyhound buses now stop at the Pilot truck stop north of Effingham.

Effingham mayor L. Keller, left, and Illinois governor Otto Kerner cut the ribbon officially opening the portion of Interstate 70 skirting Effingham in the summer of 1961. As one can see, the highway had already been open for traffic before the ribbon cutting, which took place on Illinois Routes 32 and 33, now known as Keller Drive within the city of Effingham. The city did not extend to the new road at that time, but that would eventually change. Interstate 57 was eventually routed through the area, causing the construction of trilevel interchanges on the north and south sides of Effingham. O'Connor Construction built the portion of Interstates 57 and 70 between the two trilevels for $3.6 million.

Two

EFFINGHAM CITY

The Effingham County Courthouse square used to be the place for teenagers to get their pictures taken, particularly in the 1940s, when this photograph was taken. Young Patty Porter leans against an old pump that used to be next to the cannon. The camera is facing north. Patty, daughter of highway engineer Kenneth Porter, later married John Kirby. Their daughter Karen Kirby Luchtefeld has been active in the community for many years, serving as an Effingham County board member.

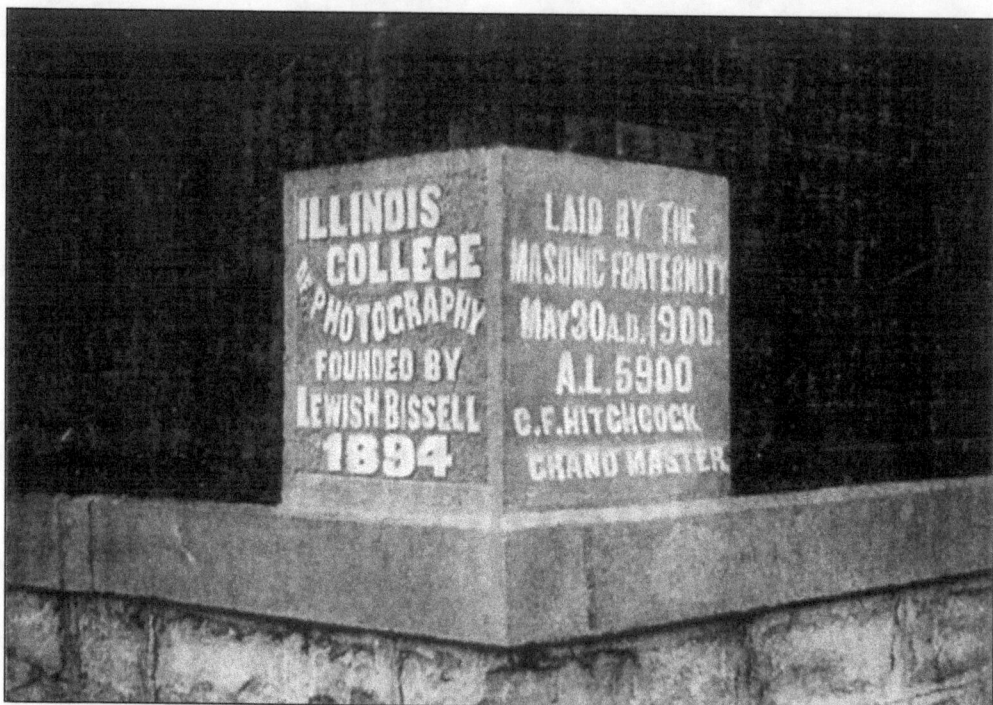

The Illinois College of Photography existed from 1900 to 1931. The college bought the old Austin College building in 1905. Garnet Hall, on the corner of Fourth Street and Wabash Avenue, has a long, storied history and has recently been renovated by its new owners.

GARNET HALL

REMBRANDT HALL

Illinois College
of
Photography.

Effingham,
Illinois.
U. S. A.

ENGRAVING HALL.

The history of Effingham County would be much poorer without Henry and Ada Kepley. Henry B. Kepley (1836–1906) was a prominent attorney in the Effingham area for many years, but he was overshadowed by wife Ada, the first female law school graduate in the United States. Ada (1847–1925) was an early crusader for women's rights and temperance.

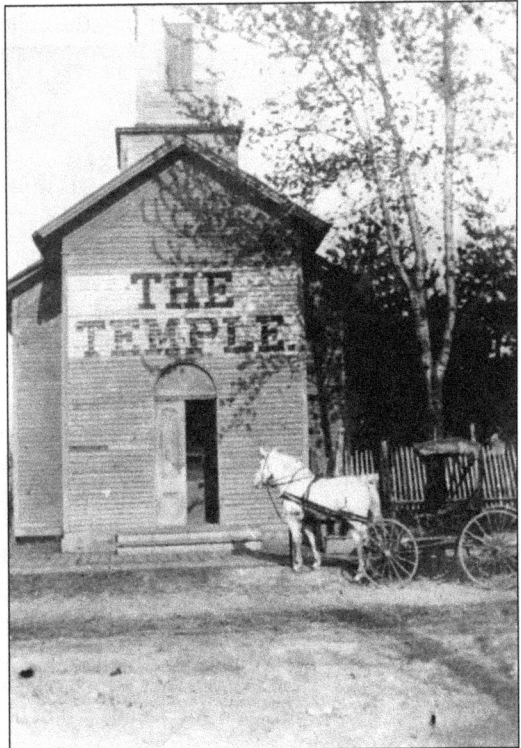

In 1884, Henry bought the old Southern Methodist Church on Fourth Street and Ada enlarged it as a public meeting place. Known as the temple, it operated as a place where the Kepleys could influence the lives of hundreds of young people. Ada closed the building after her husband Henry died in 1906.

L. H. Bissell was a prominent early photographer with a studio at 101½ East Jefferson Street, across from the courthouse. Bissell later founded the Illinois College of Photography on the south side of town. The college attracted students from around the world. While the Illinois College of Photography was headquartered in Garnet Hall, it also included Rembrandt Hall to the north. Rembrandt Hall had originally been used as a stable for the Austin family, with two apartments for those who took care of the horses. The Illinois College of Photography closed in 1931, after the Great Depression cut into the college's attendance base.

Garnet Hall was recently bought by Craig and Dominique Mueller. Dominique is an executive with Target Corporation, while Craig stays home with the couple's two daughters and supervises the home's continuing renovation. The Effingham High School building trades class began renovation years ago.

Here is a winter scene of Garnet Hall from the 1920s. Note the emptiness to the left of the home across Wabash Avenue. That area has long since been developed. A photograph from the same angle taken today would show a number of homes, reflecting that development.

A group from the Effingham Woman's Relief Corps of the Civil War Veterans poses for this picture. Those pictured include Alberta Morrison Martin (to the left of the flag) and Virginia Stevenson Morrison (to the right of the flag).

Downtown Effingham started changing in the 1950s. Here is the Emery Boerngen home on the corner of Banker Street and Washington Avenue in the mid-1950s. Clem Niebrugge's shop is to the left, while the American Legion post is partially shown to the right.

In this photograph, the Boerngen home has been torn down and work has begun on Legion Plaza.

Here is the completed Legion Plaza. The building originally housed law and insurance offices. It is now home to social service offices.

Jefferson Street was the main drag in Effingham for many decades. Above, in this 1950s shot taken from the intersection of Fourth and Jefferson Streets, businesses on the left include a Shell gas station. The Benwood Hotel, partially shown here, was directly across the street from the Shell station. The photograph below was taken about the same time from the intersection of Banker and Jefferson Streets. The First National Bank is the first building on the left, followed by the Federated Department Store, later known as Jansen's. The Ideal and Young shops are the first two businesses to the right.

Effingham's city functions were all housed in this building for many years. The police department moved into the old Kroger store in the 1970s. The city clerk's office moved into a new building on the corner of Third and Jefferson Streets in the 1990s, but the fire department stayed put until moving into a new central fire station in 2004.

Emory and Katherine Palso operated the youth recreation center, also known as "the Rec," on the whole third floor of the downtown Register Building (formerly known as the opera house) during the 1940s. This photograph was taken in 1944. The center included pool tables, a jukebox with the latest tunes to dance to, and booths to hang out in with friends. High school kids from the surrounding schools knew where they could meet their friends.

The corner of Front Street and Jefferson Avenue has hosted business for more than a century. In this photograph, taken around 1920, Coca-Cola was still a nickel and Miller's on the corner sold Old Homestead Bread. Coca-Cola was known for years as an antidote for fatigue, probably because it had cocaine in it at one time. Company founder Asa Candler took out the cocaine after passage of the Pure Food and Drug Act in 1906. This photograph is facing east, looking down Jefferson. The street has always had that jog to the left after it crosses Banker Street.

This building in the 100 block of South Banker Street served as Effingham City Hall until a new city hall was built on the site of the old Illinois Glove Factory several blocks east. The city's fire department continued to use the old building until the new central fire station was opened in 2004.

This tall cigar-shaped structure—known as the standpipe—stored Effingham's water until it was torn down in the 1970s. The Raleigh Hotel is partially shown to the right. The photograph was taken from the southeast corner of Banker Street and Fayette Avenue in the early years of the 20th century, judging from the condition of the streets.

The Gravenhorsts were business titans in Effingham during most of the 20th century. Here is Theodore S. Gravenhorst Sr., president of John Boos and Company and Gravenhorst Department Store, at the wheel of a float for the 1920 street fair. His wife Katherine is portraying Lady Liberty. They are parked in front of their home at 207 West Lawrence Avenue. Two years later, Theodore would be dead. His son and grandson later served as president of John Boos and Company.

Convicted killer Nathan Burgess breathed his last on June 18, 1875. Young Burgess had been convicted of killing a Vandalia man. Evidence released years later revealed that Burgess's father was the actual killer. The hanging of Nathan Burgess was the only public execution in the history of Effingham County.

The Pleasant Point Cafe was a downtown hangout for quite a few years in the mid-20th century. In this photograph, Lorna Jackson (left) and Dora Cox are behind the counter. Seated from front to back are officer James Haslett of the Effingham Police Department, unidentified, Wally Hewkin, and Genean Hinkleman.

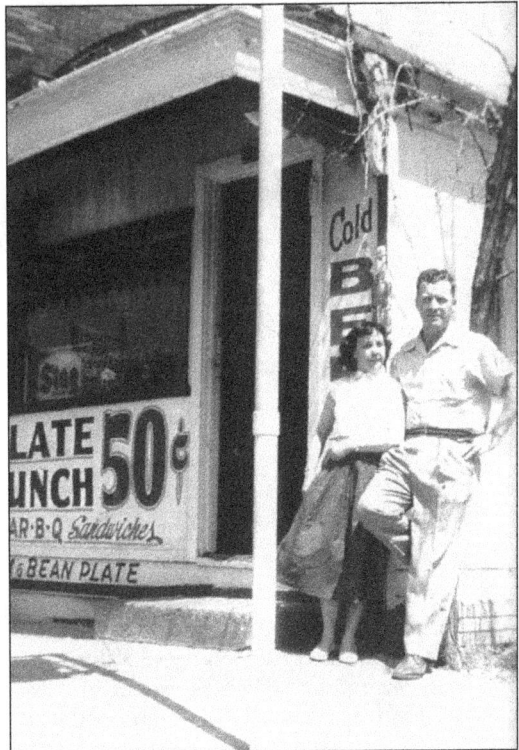

Ralph Aubrey and Lorna Jackson owned the Pleasant Point Cafe from 1953 to 1961. The café was located just north of the old Sacred Heart Catholic Church on the corner of Banker Street and Section Avenue in downtown Effingham. The Jacksons bought the café from Rex Adams in 1953 and sold it to Tom and Irma Johnston in 1961. Aubrey hired future contractor Ray Esker to be the first Dixie Creme doughnut deliveryman. David Jenkins made the doughnuts. The café was eventually converted into a full-time doughnut shop before its sale to the Johnstons.

Participants in the October 1918 parade are lining up in front of the courthouse on Jefferson Street. Today's Jefferson Avenue is one-way headed east, meaning that a legal replication of the above scene would be impossible today.

The Effingham Street Fair was popular during the early years of the 20th century. Bands played and floats were pulled down the street in those days before mass use of internal combustion engines. John B. Althoff is the man on the horse in the top hat in front of the band. This photograph was taken sometime between 1900 and 1902.

The U.S. post office in Effingham was once located at 131 West Jefferson Street, later the home of B&H Clothing. Postmaster William Austin is standing in the center of the photograph in front of the door. Harry Devore is to his left, while Fred Reichelm is to his right. Fourth and fifth from left in the first row are Frank Chamberlin and Bill Wachtel, respectively. The young carrier on the far left of the back row is unidentified, but to the right of him are Bill Kyle, Roscoe Mikeworth, and assistant postmaster John Hutchings.

Generations of young entrepreneurs have gotten their start as newspaper carriers. These guys threw the *St. Louis Post-Dispatch* and *Globe-Democrat* and are seen in a photograph believed to be from the late 1930s. From left to right are (first row) Merle E. Yemm, Ray Repking, and Elbert Fuesting; (second row) Matt Volmer, Cletus Lustig, Jim Poppelmeyer, Lawrence Repking, Vincent Koester, Fritz Grunloh, and Harry Luchtefeld.

Effingham likes its parades. In the photograph above, the Moose Lodge float passes businesses on Jefferson Street between Fourth and Fifth Streets. Below, the VFW float heads toward the Benwood Hotel in the upper right. The buildings in the upper left part of the photograph were torn down in 2005 to make room for the new Effingham County Government Center.

This was the scene at the corner of Jefferson Street and North Railroad Street. Austin Lumber Company also sold coal, ice, buggies, and implements. This photograph was taken in 1895.

Effingham had a Modern Woodmen of America lodge at one time. This early photograph shows Clarence Phillips at the far left, Willie Smith fourth from the left, and Glen Smith third from the right. Modern Woodmen was founded in 1883 and is headquartered in Rock Island.

Here is Jefferson Street around the dawn of the 20th century, if not sooner. The photographer appears to be shooting from the second story of a building on the corner of Banker and Jefferson Streets. The Effingham County Courthouse tower is visible at the top of the photograph, above the Welcome sign.

The Liberty Bell stopped in Effingham as part of a nationwide campaign culminating in the 1893 World's Colombian Exposition of Chicago. The bell, of course, made it back home to its permanent resting place in Philadelphia.

The Benwood Hotel was a downtown institution for decades. Built in 1923 as a three-story structure, a fourth floor was later added. The photograph above faces west from the corner of Fourth and Jefferson Streets, soon after the hotel opened. Illinois Route 11 was designated on state maps until the late 1930s, even though its route was taken over by U.S. Route 40 in 1925. According to Wikipedia, if the federal government should ever decommission U.S. Route 40 in Illinois, it would revert to Illinois Route 11 from the Mississippi River to the Indiana state line, a 200-mile route. In the photograph below, the fourth floor has been added. The hotel boomed during World War II, but was thrown off the beaten path when the interstate highways were completed in the 1960s. The hotel lingered on until the early 1980s, however, when the building was converted into the Effingham County Office Building. It remains in use for a variety of county offices.

Oak Ridge Cemetery predates the city of Effingham. The first grave in the new cemetery was 50-year-old Mary Moore, laid to rest on July 27, 1853. The cemetery has grown considerably since then and is typically the venue for one of the city's Memorial Day observances. This undated photograph shows the front entrance to the cemetery in its early years.

Many of Effingham's Catholic residents are buried in St. Anthony Cemetery on the north edge of town. The cemetery was established on land donated to the church by Mr. and Mrs. William Althoff in 1857. The first recorded burial was Josephus Brown in 1859. Many of Effingham's most prominent families have relatives buried there.

42

Lake Kanagga was built to supply water for the Vandalia Railroad lines in the late 1800s. It was also a popular recreation spot in the Effingham area for much of the 20th century, particularly in the first half. It was located off U.S. Route 40, west of the city. Its owners eventually filled in the lake, and no traces of it remain.

In the days before air conditioning, folks beat the heat any way they could. Here is a group enjoying Salt Creek, east of Effingham, during a summer afternoon in 1907.

43

A lone boater enjoys Lake Sara, northwest of Effingham. The lake was built in the 1950s by impounding Blue Point Creek. While its primary purpose has always been as a secondary water source for Effingham, the Effingham Water Authority has overseen development of numerous subdivisions and businesses in the lake area. The lake was dedicated on November 10, 1957, and named for Sara Everhart, whose husband chaired the water authority.

One always knew when school was about to start in Effingham during the 1950s and 1960s. That is because downtown merchants would block off Jefferson Street for the annual downtown garage sale. This photograph is believed to be from the mid-1960s, after Effingham State Bank got its digital clock, shown at left. Business to the left, or south, side of the street at the time were the bank, B&H Clothing, a newsstand, and Maurice Rickleman's law office. On the right, or north, side were the Jansen's Department Store, Thomas Shop, Washington Savings Bank, Ealy Realty, Little Chef, John Green department store, National Studio, and Model Ladies Shop. Buildings on the north side of the street to the right of Fifth Street were demolished several years ago to make room for the Effingham County Government Center.

Many Greyhound bus riders enjoyed a meal at the Pleasant Point Cafe on Banker Street and Section Avenue during the late 1940s. The bus depot was at the Raleigh Hotel across the street. Pleasant Point was particularly known for its home-cooked plate lunches.

The Grand Central Hotel was Effingham's first. Located on the northwest corner of Banker and Jefferson Streets, the Grand Central lost some of its luster when the Benwood opened in 1923. Nevertheless, the building has endured and is now occupied by a bicycle shop.

Three

EFFINGHAM BUSINESS

Isaac Francis Morrison
served in both the Civil and
Spanish-American Wars.
Between wars, Morrison was a
brick mason who helped build
Central School and many other
brick buildings in town.

Chester Knitting Mills opened its Effingham plant in 1918 on the corner of Third and Jefferson Streets. The mill employed between 100 and 200 people at any given time during its 10-year stay in the city. After Chester moved out in the late 1920s, the Illinois Glove Company moved in and occupied the building for many years. The building was later torn down to make room for the new Effingham City Hall.

John Boos and Company is one of the most venerable businesses in Effingham. Now located at the corner of Willow Street and Fayette Avenue, blacksmith Conrad Boos founded the business in 1887 in the back of his blacksmith shop at 406 West Jefferson Street. Boos started out making butcher blocks for meat markets and die blocks for the leather industry. Since then, the business has become best known for the manufacture of laminated blocks, although it makes a number of other items.

The Effingham Canning Factory was located south of the Vandalia (later Pennsylvania) Railroad tracks on East Fayette Avenue. The members in this group picture are unidentified, but it can be surmised that the photograph was taken in the 1920s because of the bobbed hair favored by many of the female employees.

The Court House Cafe served diners across the street from the Effingham County Courthouse for a number of years. Employees in this photograph, from about 1940 or 1941, include, from left to right, (first row) Vera Baker, unidentified, owner Rex Adams, Treva Ryan, unidentified, Louella Worman, unidentified, and Connie ?; (second row) Verena Wendt, Marion Webster, Helen Hampton, unidentified, Beulah Brown, ? Pendley, Lula Martin, and unidentified.

The Raleigh Hotel was strategically located at the intersection of U.S. Routes 40 and 45 for a number of years. A large auto-parts store is presently located on that site. The hotel also housed the local taxi company. Seen here from left to right are (first row) hotel assistant manager Hilda Stumborg, manager Henry Mettzer, and Ada Henry Currier; (second row) taxi owner Ross Webking, taxi driver Ross Nelson, clerks Holly Snyder and Harry Boehm, and taxi driver Richard Loy. This photograph was taken in 1946.

If this aerial shot was taken today, it would be dominated by Village Square Mall. But this shot was taken in 1968, several years before the mall was built. The building that appears to be in the middle of the field is an auction barn. Mid-State Lumber is in the top center of the picture, while one can see part of the sprawling Norge plant. At the time of this picture, the plant covered nearly 13 acres under roof and employed about 1,600 people. Fedders Corporation later bought the plant. Over the years, the operation dwindled. Production was stopped several years ago, leaving only a handful of office employees.

How times have changed. At 1:00 p.m. (as shown by the Effingham County Courthouse clock at the top of the photograph), the Sur brothers, Lawrence and Ed, were selling gas at eight gallons for $1 at their station on the corner of Third and Jefferson Streets. The store was later taken over by Ray and Dave Probst, who operated it until the City of Effingham bought the property for parking and tore down the station after more than 70 years in operation.

Lolama "Lamie" (1908–1975) and Thelma Bushue Keller (1910–1996) were Effingham business icons for more than a generation in the mid-20th century. Here is the second service station owned by the couple, a DX station on the corner of South Banker Street and Wernsing Avenue that opened in the late 1930s.

Here are Lamie and Thelma Keller in their first service station on Banker Street at the south end of town in the early 1930s. As L. Keller, Lamie was Effingham's mayor in the 1960s. Their son Charles F. (Chuck) Keller was later an Illinois state representative.

The Kellers later opened this Shell station and Ramada Inn at the junction of Keller Drive and Interstates 57 and 70. The complex opened on November 16, 1963. Its grand opening was delayed after the assassination of Pres. John F. Kennedy six days later. The hotel has since been remodeled to become the Thelma Keller Convention Center.

Lamie and Thelma were not the only Kellers involved in the Effingham business community. Here is Lamie's dad, Charles Alexander Keller (left), and Charles's teenage son (Lamie's older brother) Gayland Hubert Keller at the counter of their produce store around 1921. The store was located on South Banker Street, two doors north of the old National Hotel. Gayland, who looks like he would rather be doing something else in this picture, preferred to be known by his middle name and was later known professionally as H. G. Keller.

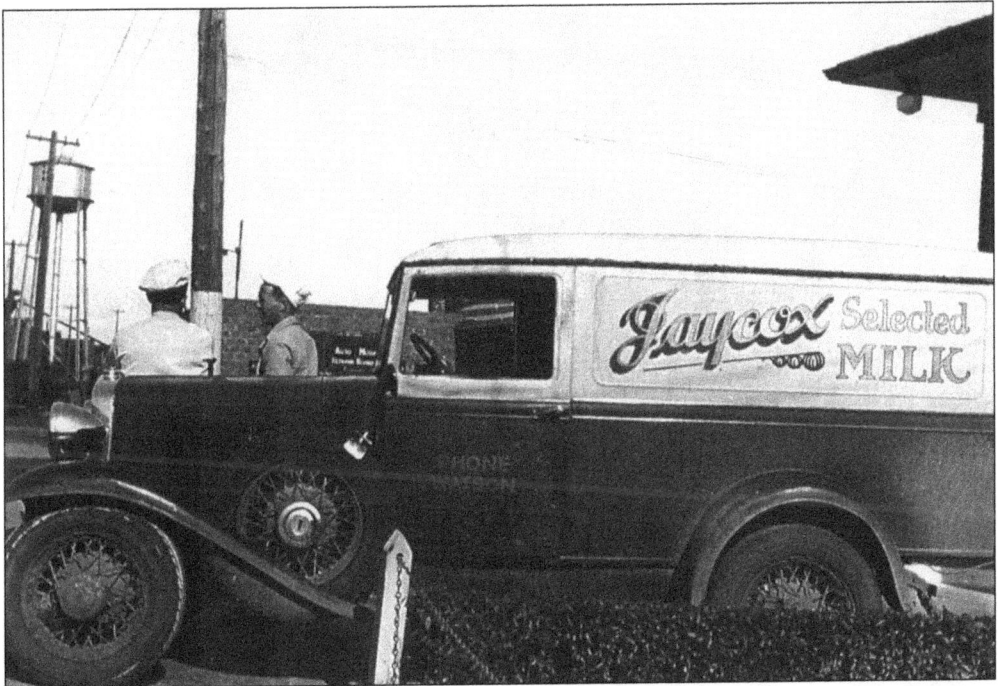

Here are Lamie Keller, left, and Chuck Jaycox visiting outside Keller's filling station sometime in the 1930s. Jaycox Dairy started out in Watson and then moved to Effingham soon after this photograph was taken. The Jaycox family sold the dairy in 1947. Chuck moved to Florida in the early 1960s.

Hubert Keller eventually went into the furniture business. Here is an aerial shot of Keller's Town and Country on U.S. Route 40 between Effingham and Teutopolis. The 40,000-square-foot store was opened in 1947, burned in 1984, and was rebuilt as a 30,000-square-foot store. It was closed in 2001 and now houses the Effingham offices of Catholic Charities, as well as a food pantry and used-goods store.

Henry H. Dust operated Dusty's Wholesale Accessories and Dusty's Tire Service during the 1920s. Shown here at the corner of Third Street and Fayette Avenue are, from left to right, Everette Dueker, Henry H. Dust, and Henry L. Dust. Henry L. opened an auto-parts store with his son Clarence in 1929. The business thrives to this day, having undergone a recent expansion in which it took over space formerly occupied by the Raleigh Hotel and Effingham City Hall.

A. H. "Dash" Dust owned Dust's Service Store for many years next door to Dust and Son Auto Parts in the 100 block of South Banker Street.

Theodore Hoffman Post 1769 of the VFW was organized on November 27, 1929, by Wendell Harris. The post was named for Effingham resident Theodore Hoffman, who was killed in World War I. A post home on South Fourth Street Road was donated by Hoffman's mother in 1933. The post has since moved into new quarters in roughly the same location and is still active in the community.

Feuerborn Manufacturing Company was founded by Conrad Feuerborn in 1878. Feuerborn had been asked to make some furniture in his cabinet shop for a local church. The business blossomed and was later moved to 202 North Willow Street, where it remained until closing in the 1970s. This photograph shows the Willow Street building, built in 1924.

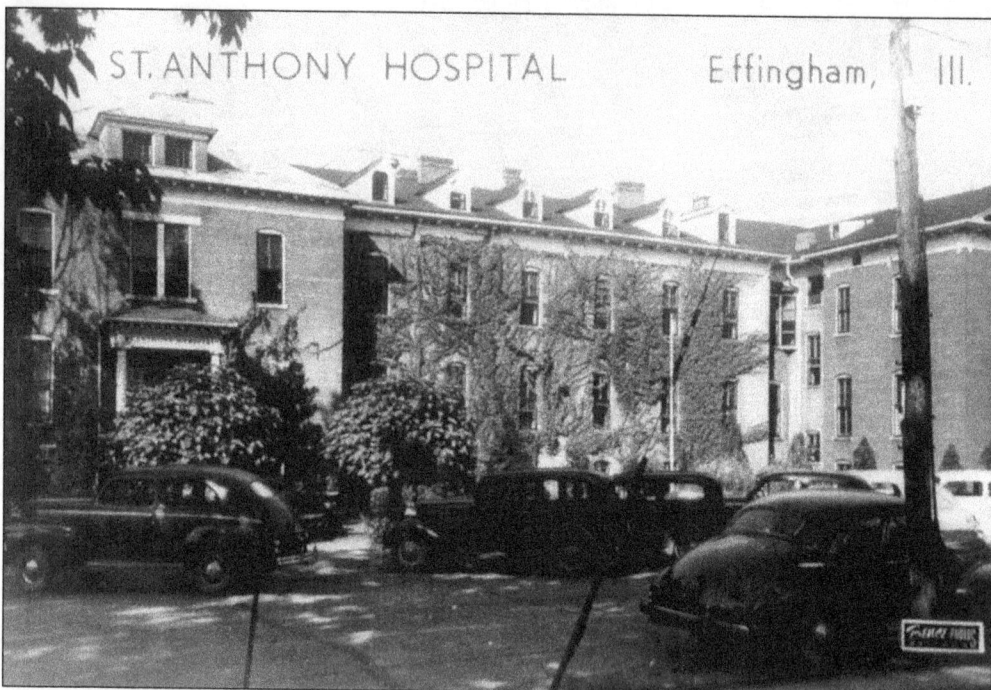

ST. ANTHONY HOSPITAL   Effingham,   Ill.

From a small healing ministry started by three German immigrant nuns in 1875, St. Anthony Hospital grew into a thriving health-care facility by the time this postcard was printed in the 1940s. The hospital cornerstone was laid in 1877, and additions were built in 1917 and 1924.

Disaster struck St. Anthony Hospital on April 4, 1949. In a tragedy that touched the world, 77 people died in a fire that destroyed the old hospital. The fire started in a laundry chute.

Here are the remains of the old St. Anthony Hospital after the 1949 fire was doused. The Hospital Sisters of St. Francis treated patients in a small building on the grounds for nearly five years until a new hospital was built.

The new St. Anthony's Memorial Hospital has stood tall over north central Effingham since its opening in 1954. The new hospital was completed and opened on February 2 of that year. Since then, Effingham has grown into a regional medical center with many medical specialties available in the area. The hospital is shown here as it appeared soon after its opening.

It is 1:55 p.m. on April 1, 1941, and the staff at Tolch Grocery Store, at 505 South Maple Street, is lined up for a photograph. The fellow at far left is unidentified, but after him from left to right are Mary Alice Morgan, Clifford Stephens, William Tolch Jr., Leo Reis, and William Tolch Sr. The Tolches were also involved in banking during the mid-20th century.

The Stephens Food Market was one of three Sell-Rite stores in Effingham during the mid-20th century. Located on St. Louis Avenue near St. Anthony Catholic Church, the store was closed in the early 1980s.

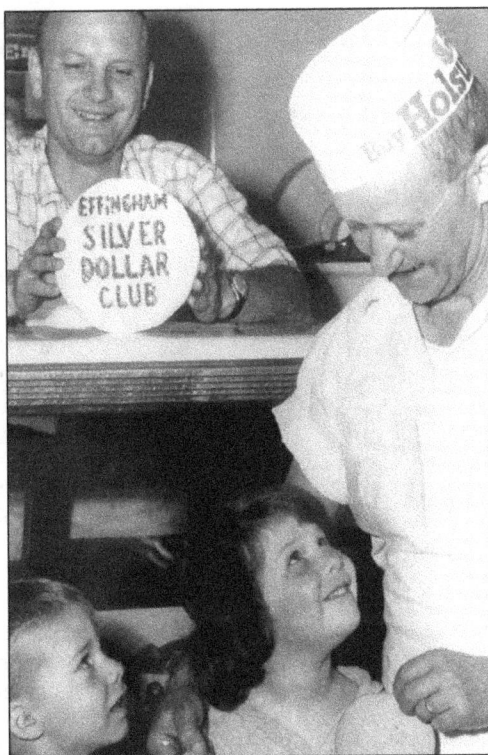

The Effingham Chamber of Commerce had a Silver Dollar Club around 1960. In this photograph, Jack Thies stands behind the meat counter, while butcher Ernie Niccum gives a pert young lady a piece of bologna as a young boy looks on. Clarence and Ed Thies opened their first grocery store in 1921, right across National Avenue from the Pennsylvania Railroad (now CSX) tracks. The original store even had a soda fountain. Niccum began working for the Thies family in the late 1930s and stayed with the store until his death around 1980.

The Heart Jewelry business was owned by George Timperman, who always seemed to have a cigar in his mouth. The store shown here was located in the 100 block of West Jefferson Street in the late 1930s. After the Heart Theatre opened on the 100 block of East Jefferson Street in 1940, Timperman moved his shop next door to the theater. Also shown in this picture is the office door of Dr. J. R. Raney, a longtime dentist (and Effingham mayor) whose offices were upstairs from the jewelry store.

Kershner Radio and Electric was owned by brothers Joe and Dave Kershner. Their original location, shown here in the late 1940s, was on Section Avenue between Fifth and Banker Streets. The brothers eventually moved their business around the corner to a location on Fifth Street. Joe handled the electronic portion of the business, while Dave took care of the refrigeration end.

Here is the Sanitary Milk Producers plant, at 505 South Willow Street, sometime after 1957. The original 50-by-150-foot milk plant was built in 1901 as the American Condensed Milk Company. Pevely Dairy bought the building in 1953 but sold it to Sanitary in 1957. Sanitary later merged into Mid-America Dairymen. By that time, the building was 200 by 300 feet and housed a railroad spur in the front of the building. The building was torn down on May 19, 1992.

Roemer's Laundry, at 121 West Jefferson Street, was more than just a laundry. During a period of time when most people only bathed once a week, Roemer's had facilities for bathing as well as commercial laundry. This photograph was likely taken in the last decade of the 19th century. It appeared in the city's 50th anniversary book published in 1903.

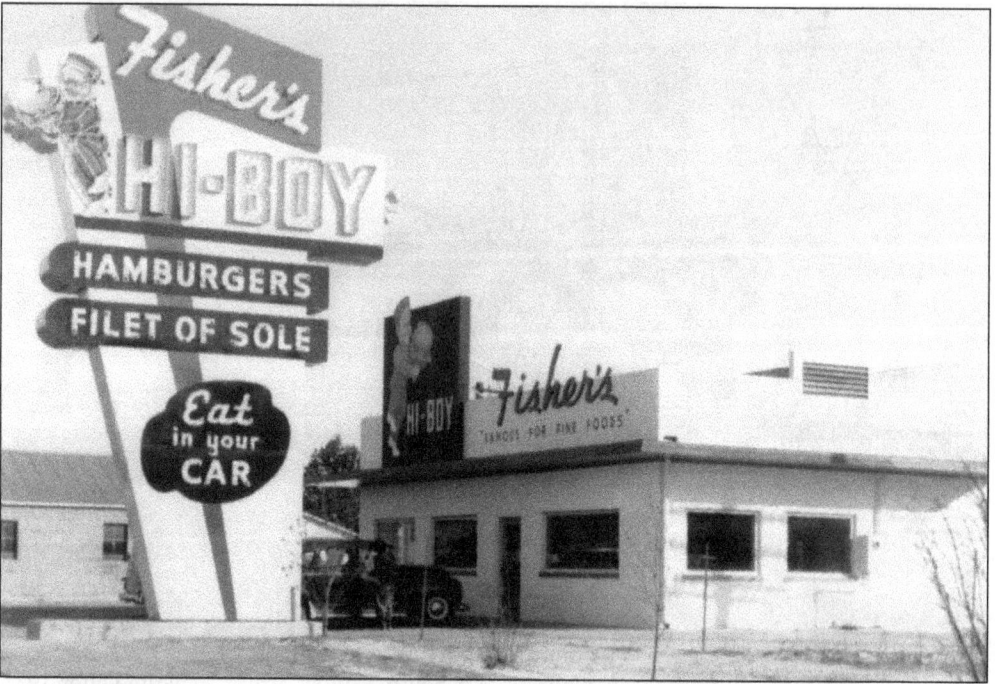

Fisher's Hi-Boy was a major hangout for Effingham teens in the mid-20th century. It was located on East Fayette Avenue. It was known for its special hamburgers and fish sandwiches.

Bartscht Memorial Library, 110 Washington Avenue, was built in 1948 to serve the needs of Effingham residents. It was replaced by the current Helen Matthes Library, located a block north, in the 1960s.

Four

SCHOOLS AND CHURCHES

St. Anthony of Padua Catholic Church was built on the corner of Third Street and St. Louis Avenue in 1873, although the church has been in existence since 1858. This photograph was undoubtedly taken some time after Third Street was designated U.S. Route 45 in 1926. Note the highway sign in the lower right of the photograph. St. Anthony church was completely renovated for its centennial celebration in 1958 and celebrated its sesquicentennial in 2008. The building is particularly sturdy because hand-hewn slabs of quarried rock form the base of each pillar.

The old Methodist Episcopal Church in Beecher City was organized as the Olive Branch Methodist Church on the Effingham-Shelby county line north of Beecher City. The building shown here was moved to its present site in 1887. The church moved out of the building in 1972, after the Methodist Episcopal and United Brethren churches merged in 1966. It is now the Lonnie Tull residence.

This Methodist Episcopal church was built in 1876 to serve Watson area Methodists. It had been part of the Ewington circuit until 1883, when it joined the Mason circuit.

Here is the Elliottstown Church of Christ as it stood in the 1970s. Now closed, the church had a long history in this tiny Lucas Township community. Originally known as the Christian Church of Elliottstown, the church was originally housed in the old schoolhouse, then the Baptist church, before moving into its own building in 1872. A new building, shown here, was built in 1919. Services were discontinued at the church some years ago, although the building still stands as a private residence.

St. Rose of Lima Catholic Church has been a cornerstone of the Montrose area for more than 100 years. The building shown here was built in 1879. A newer building was built in 1959 and dedicated the following year.

Centenary United Methodist Church has served the Effingham area since 1865. The building shown here, on South Fifth Street in Effingham, housed the church from 1896 to 1955. It was just south of Central School. The building is no longer there, although the Church of God used the building for several years after the Methodists built their new church.

LUTHERAN CHURCH

Even though Effingham is most often associated with Catholicism, Lutherans have a long history in the city as well. St. John's Lutheran Church has been serving the community since 1866. The present building, shown here, was built in 1935. St. John's has been associated with the Lutheran Church-Missouri Synod since 1881. Services were originally in German, but English began to be mixed in with the old language around 1911 and increased during the World War I period later that decade. St. Paul Church was built for the English speaking but later merged with St. John's when German was finally discontinued in the early 1900s.

Blue Point Baptist Church is on the old Moccasin Road about five miles northwest of Effingham. The church building, shown here, was built in 1877 by a group of local farmers that had met in each other's homes for the previous 30 years. Circuit-riding preachers came to the church once a month for meetings that lasted all weekend. The church still thrives today in the same building shown here, although the impoundment that created Lake Sara in the 1950s took away much of the nearby farmland.

St. Mary's Help of Christians Catholic Church has served the spiritual needs of the Green Creek community for more than a century. This photograph was taken in 1907, after the church had been organized for nearly 50 years. Father Frauenhofer organized the church in 1857. He left the area after a couple of years, and Franciscans from Teutopolis took over the church. The first building was erected a few years later.

Here is St. Aloysius Catholic Church as it looked in 1907. More than 100 years later, St. Aloysius still serves Catholics in the Bishop Creek area between Teutopolis and Dieterich. The church was organized in 1859. The present building was completed in 1894. From its inception, the church has been staffed by Franciscan priests from Teutopolis.

Here is an 1894 photograph of the student and teacher population at Loy School near Watson. From the looks of this December 11 photograph, it appears that Loy School served students from early childhood through the teen years. Loy remained open until the 1948 formation of Unit 40 forced many old rural schools to close. Loy was one of 80 rural elementary districts abolished when the unit system of educational administration was begun.

Here is a school picture from the late 1920s at Dexter School near Altamont. Those identified are Irvin Tucker, Velma Devore, Bessie Myers, Henry Myers, Raymond Devore, Arthur Devore, Gehl Devore, Nadine Tucker, Edna Keplar, Roy Young, John Sutter, Lloyd Sheehan, Gerald Van Alst, Harold Devore, Clyde Smith, Frank Keplar, Faye Young, Cosilda Van Alst, Faye Miller, Carrie Miller, Helen Lathrop, Dorothy Myers, Naomi Tucker, Thelma Lathrop, Lester Keplar, Ed Tucker, Cherry Higgins Tucker, Forrest Keplar, Lawrence Devore, Paul Smith, and Earl Young.

The class of 1922 at Moccasin High School includes, from left to right, (first row) Clarissa Jane Flenniken; (second row) Lolo Holley, Hazel Harrison, Dorothy Younger, Naomi Johnstone, Bessie Holley, Edna Strus, and Birdie Doty; (third row) Jesse Doty, Dietrich Boehner, Oscar Wurl, Fred Homann, and Glen Clawson. Moccasin High School students only attended a two-year program. Those seeking additional high school education could then attend Altamont High School, which did have a four-year program by then. Several county towns also had three-year schools, which were disbanded when the unit system of education was instituted in 1948.

It is recess time at Banner School, near Shumway, around 1910. Banner, located at the intersection of county roads 1050E and 1950N, was closed as a result of the massive school consolidation effort of 1948, in which 80 elementary school districts were folded into five larger school districts.

Students line up for a class picture at Oak Grove School near Altamont around 1900. Oak Grove District 63 was closed by consolidation in 1948.

Here is the brand-spanking-new Teutopolis High School, completed in 1929. The photographer is standing near U.S. Route 40, looking southwest toward the new school. The school has since been added on to several times. Nonetheless, the original building still stands and is in use.

St. Anthony School
Effingham, Illinois

St. Anthony School has served thousands of Effingham schoolchildren since Franciscan priests built a two-room school in 1862. By the time this postcard was published in the 1950s, the St. Anthony grade and high schools were in the same building. The gymnasium, foreground, was built in 1949. A new high school was opened in 1967, and a new grade school is under construction adjacent to the school shown here.

Central Grade School was built in 1894 on the corner of Fifth Street and Fayette Avenue, just south of downtown Effingham. This building was perhaps best known as the home of Effingham High School until a new school was built in 1940 on the west end of town. Central then housed first through eighth graders, until it was closed in 1979. This photograph faces southwest across Fayette. After the school was torn down, the water fountain in the center of this photograph was moved to Community Park.

Effingham High School students moved into a more modern high school on Henrietta Street in 1940. This building served as the high school until a new school was built across the street in the late 1990s. The old high school was then converted into a junior high school.

Teutopolis High School was built in 1929 and expanded around 1950. Here is a photograph taken after the expansion.

Five

TEUTOPOLIS

The man on the left holds a special place in Teutopolis history. George Deymann (or Deyman) was renowned for his wooden shoe making during a long life that lasted from 1849 to 1937. Deymann made the shoes out of lindenwood and sold them for 75¢ to $1.25 per pair. Toward the end of his life, old Deymann still enjoyed a beer. The young man pouring him a brew is believed to be George Wernsing (1899–1966), who was married to Deymann's granddaughter Florence Busse.

Flour Mill, Teutopolis, Ill.

Siemer Milling Company has its roots in the early days of Teutopolis, when town founder Clemens Uptmor started a wind-driven flour mill. In 1882, Uptmor, son Clemens Jr., and son-in-law Joseph Siemer built a steam-driven mill on the block west of the old St. Joseph's College. First known as Uptmor and Siemer, the mill was producing 300 barrels of flour, 400 bushels of meal, and 200 bags of feed per day by the early years of the 20th century. The first picture shows the back of the mill (facing what are now the CSX railroad tracks). After Clemens Uptmor Sr. died in 1893 and Clemens Uptmor Jr. followed him 12 years later, Joseph Siemer continued in the milling business. The name was changed from Uptmor and Siemer to Siemer Milling on October 6, 1906. Siemer Milling Company celebrated its 125th anniversary in the fall of 2007. Joseph's great-grandson Rick is the latest Siemer to operate the milling facility. The second picture is taken from a postcard printed around 1955.

Siemer Milling Co.
Teutopolis, Ill.

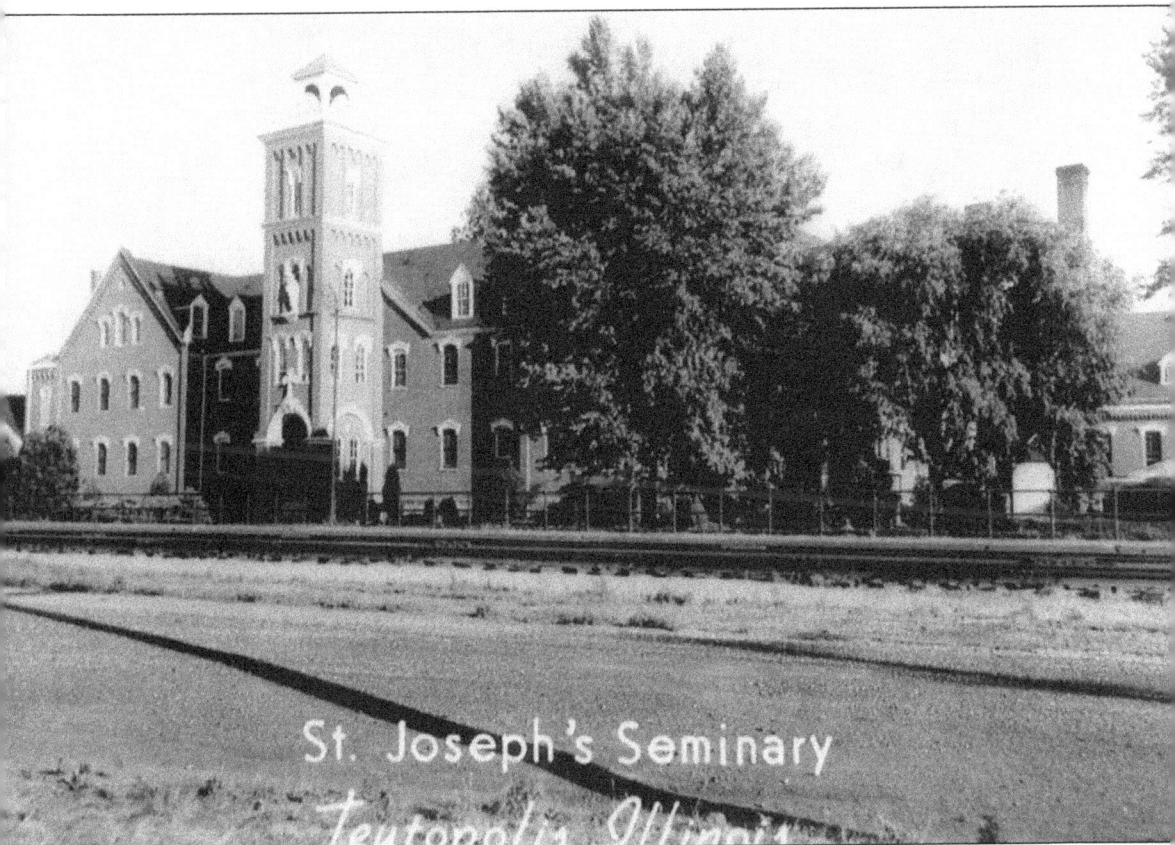

St. Joseph's Seminary

Teutopolis, Illinois

St. Joseph's Seminary was a Teutopolis institution for more than 100 years. Construction began in 1861. The last novitiates took their vows in 1969. The Knights of Columbus bought the building after the seminary closed and used it as a club, teen center, and apartments before most of it was torn down in the 1970s. A south wing built as a dormitory in the 1940s was torn down several years later. All that remains of the old seminary is the tower, shown here in the left of the photograph.

Weber Clothing and Jewelry has a long history in downtown Teutopolis. Founded by Henry J. Weber in 1892 as a clothing store, the store later expanded into jewelry after Henry's son Charles joined the business. Charles's sons Henry Lee and Donald later operated the store for many years, during which time the store expanded greatly. The business is still in the family after 116 years. Both of these photographs were taken from roughly the same part of the store, albeit many years apart. In the first picture, founder Henry J. Weber (with mustache) stands at the front right. It is anybody's guess who the other gentlemen are. Judging from the gas lamp hanging from the ceiling, this photograph was probably taken around 1910. In the second picture, an older Henry J. Weber is waiting on unidentified customers at the counter, around 1935. By then, the store had electric lamps.

By the 1960s, Charles's sons Donald "Duck" Weber and Henry "Pelee" Weber had taken over the store. Here they show off the beards they grew for the village's quasquicentennial celebration in 1964. The young man in the aisle is Don Weber Jr., then aged 16. Duck's son Kurt and Pelee's son Tony currently own the store.

The Wessel family has been involved in the grocery business for nearly 100 years. But groceries were sold on what is now the corner of Main Street and Pearl Street from the time Teutopolis was founded in 1839. Founding father Clemens Uptmor opened a store on the corner in 1863 in a new building that remained virtually unchanged until a new store was finally built in 1987. Henry Wessel and Louis Fulle bought the store in 1915. In this photograph, from left to right, Louis Fulle, employee Bill Tolch (who later opened his own store in Effingham), and Henry Wessel pose for the camera not long after they bought the store. As time went on, the second generation of Wessels and Fulles started taking part in the store's operation.

In the 1930s, when this photograph was taken, young Edwin "Sodie" Fulle was working at the store and learning from his dad, Louis Fulle, and Henry Wessel how to run a successful grocery operation. Sodie Fulle and Henry's son Barney Wessel later co-owned the store until Sodie sold his share to Barney in 1970.

Barney was still running Wessel's from the same location well into the 1980s, when this photograph was taken. Barney's son John started working at the store in 1974, returning home full-time upon graduation from Southern Illinois University–Carbondale in 1983. Father and son built a new store behind the old store in 1987, after which the old store was torn down and Barney retired. John continues to operate the store.

Teutopolis's history has been intertwined with the old National Road since its founding in 1839. Also known as U.S. Route 40 or Main Street, the street long predates its designation as part of the national highway system in the 1920s. The camera is facing west on a sunny August day in 1917.

Ben and Bill Weber were the original Weber Brothers. They were the seventh and eighth children of Joseph and Catherine Weber. Their oldest brother, Henry J., founded Weber's Clothing (now Weber's Clothing and Jewelry). Ben opened a hardware store in 1899, with younger brother Bill joining him shortly thereafter. In this photograph, the brothers are leaning against a tractor tire not too many years before Ben's death in 1947.

Here is Bill Weber behind the counter at Weber Brothers, sometime around 1940.

Weber Brothers would have annual spring sale days to show off new machinery. This scene appears to be from sometime in the second decade of the 20th century. The stairwell on the west side of the building led to living quarters for the Ben Weber family.

Trees still lined Main Street in this shot of the Weber Brothers facade from sometime around 1935.

Most of the trees were gone by the time this shot was taken around 1950. After World War II, the store started selling those newfangled Frigidaire refrigerators.

SCISSORS
SHEARS

KEEN·KUTTER

POCKET
KNIVES

The original Weber Brothers started working their children into the business well before this shot of cousins Leo "Buddy" Weber and Viola Weber Tolch was taken around 1950. The photograph can be dated in part from the presence of fluorescent lighting fixtures, installed after World War II.

After Ben died in 1947, the family split the business into two. Ben's sons stayed put with Weber Brothers Equipment, while Bill's family moved across the street to establish Weber Implement. This shot was taken around 1955, with Albert Adams and Bill Weber Jr. behind the counter.

It seemed like everybody had a nickname in Teutopolis. Three of Ben Weber's sons were nicknamed Buddy, Boots, and Peanuts. In this photograph of Weber Brothers' employees from around 1950, from left to right are Bernard "Deafie" Zehner, Clarence "Tater" Brumleve, Roman Lidy, Jim "Whitey" Borries, unidentified, Jim Burford, Leonard Funneman, and somebody remembered these days only as Smitty.

This aerial shot from perhaps 1950 shows St. Francis church on the lower left with the rectory behind it. St. Joseph's Seminary is in the upper right on the other side of the Pennsylvania Railroad tracks.

A lone buggy is westbound on Main Street. The St. Francis church steeple is visible through the winter-bare trees. It is unclear what the banner says, but there were probably many such banners strung across main roads in the days before radio or television.

Here is the 200 block of West Main Street in 1957. From left are the Mary Hutmacher home that once housed a millinery shop, the restaurant and residence of Albert Krone, and a barn that Weber Brothers used for machinery assembly. The J. B. Esker Construction Company has replaced all these structures.

Sylvester Pruemer poses with a pool cue in Braun's Pool Room sometime around 1930. Ambrose "Braunie" Braun (pronounced like brown) and his wife, the former Agnes Lidy, owned some sort of tavern, restaurant, or poolroom in downtown Teutopolis for many years.

Six

ALTAMONT/BEECHER CITY

Annabelle Bryant Smith is the woman in this photograph, taken sometime between 1905 and 1910. The man and boy are unidentified. The photograph was taken in front of Annabelle's home in Beecher City.

Hogge Brothers Hardware Store was a Beecher City institution for many years. In this picture, the Hogges (as well as most of the rest of the town) are celebrating the first day Majestic Ranges are available at the store. W. W. Hogge is standing to the left of the sign, Mamie Hogge is in front of the door, with Grandma Hogge next to her. The photograph was probably taken sometime around 1914 or 1915.

It is April 12, 1913, and the Hogges are celebrating something. There is even a band. Just as many towns had their own baseball teams, many had community bands in the days before radio or television.

Binders were invented in 1872 and quickly became a popular improvement on the mechanical reaper. It was well into the 20th century before combines made the binder obsolete. Here Hogge Brothers Hardware in Beecher City is having a binder rally one summer in the second decade of the 20th century. Partners W. W. and George Hogge are standing in front, while Leah Hogge is the little girl in the white dress and Dorothy Hogge is sitting on a binder.

Disaster struck the Hogges in March 1921 when fire destroyed the old store. In this shot, only spools of metal wire survived the blaze.

Hogge's rebuilt after the 1921 fire and stayed open for many decades thereafter. In these pictures taken around 1950, one can see the front of the new store.

Hogge's was still going strong in September 1950, when this photograph was taken. By this time, the second generation was running the store. From left to right are Byron Little, W. B. "Junior" Hogge, Leah Hogge Little, and Sammie Syfert.

Here is the loading dock at Hogge's at the south side of their store.

The Effingham County Fair has been in continuous operation at the Altamont fairgrounds since 1946. The new fair probably reminded a few old-timers of the Altamont Agricultural Association fair that ran from 1906 to 1917. Here is the grandstand for the old fair, known then as an amphitheater.

RAIL ROAD DEPOT   ALTAMONT ILL.   H H BREGSTONE ST LOUIS

Like many small towns in Illinois, Altamont was a key stop on several railroads in the late 19th and early 20th centuries. The building on the left is the Pennsylvania Railroad depot, while the building on the right is a switching tower that was rendered obsolete by automated switching devices. The depot was staffed full-time until 1970 and on a part-time basis for several years thereafter. The depot was torn down in the mid-1990s, while the switching tower was torn down in the early 1950s.

Here is Railroad Street before a 1905 fire decimated much of the back part of the block.

CONCRETE BLOCK FACTORY—C. D. YOUNG—SHUMWAY, ILL.

PHOTO BY LEITZELL.

C. D. Young operated a block factory two and a half miles north of the Dexter community, northeast of Altamont, southeast of Beecher City, and south of Shumway. This 1908 photograph shows concrete blocks drying in the sun. The water used to spray the bricks to keep them from drying too fast in the sun was held in the round tank in the center of the photograph. Blocks were manufactured in the barn behind the stacks of drying blocks. Young also manufactured ornamental concrete for fences and yard decorations.

Altamont had a Fourth of July parade for decades until it was discontinued in 1959. Shown in this 1926 photograph on Washington Street are pharmacist Otto Moll, Bertha Weiler, and her husband Arthur. The Weilers owned the Rexall drugstore, and Moll was their pharmacist. Dr. Leseman, a dentist, had an office upstairs from the drugstore. Other buildings on the block were the U.S. post office, Buddy's Soda Shop, H. C. Wendt Jewelry, and G. W. Gwinn's John Deere shop.

Here is a look on the east side of Second Street in the second decade of the 20th century. A haberdashery is on the far left, with a feed store in the middle, and Charles Durst's drugstore to the right. Many downtown buildings had apartments on the second floor.

Seven

OTHER PLACES

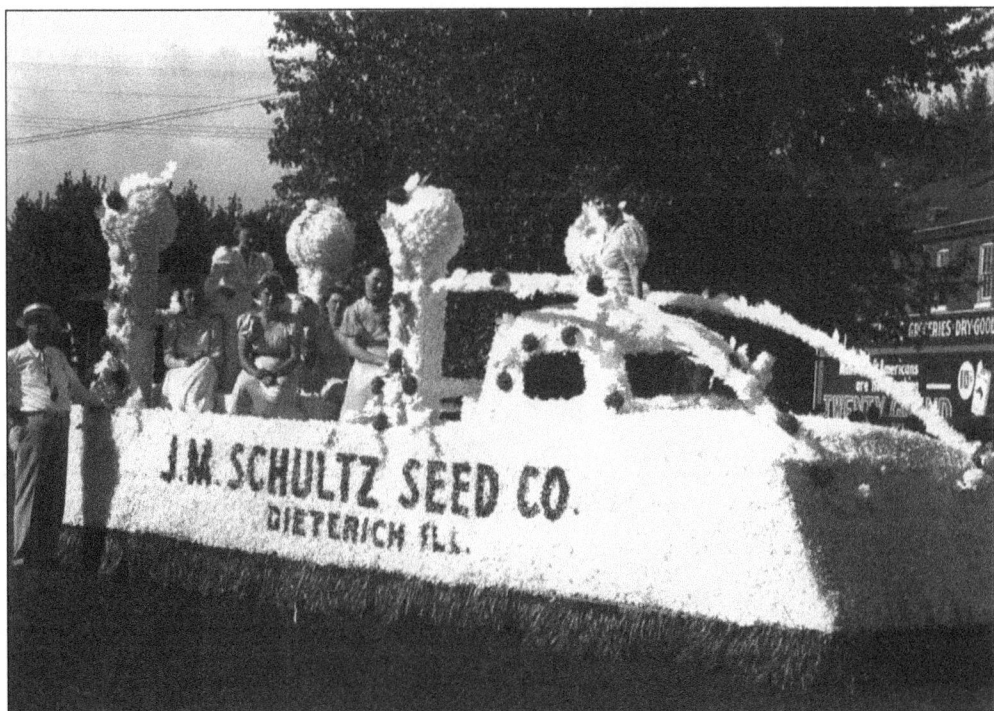

The Schultzes still found time for fun, despite the pressures of running a successful business. In this 1939 photograph, John M. Schultz is shown standing alongside a float for the 1939 Teutopolis centennial parade. Seated from left to right are daughter-in-law Marian Brumleve Schultz and daughters Esther and Alberta. The other ladies are unidentified. John M. and Elizabeth Schultz raised their children in Teutopolis, even though the business was located in Dieterich.

Here is the scene at Schultz's hardware store in 1907. August Schultz married his wife, Mary, in 1871, and they had seven sons. Two of the boys, Frank (born 1875) and John (born 1878), opened a hardware store in 1903. Shown here from left to right are (first row) August's wife Mary, granddaughter Helen, August, and son John M. The two salesmen in the back row are unidentified; the young fellow to their left is Ferd Althoff, who later bought the store.

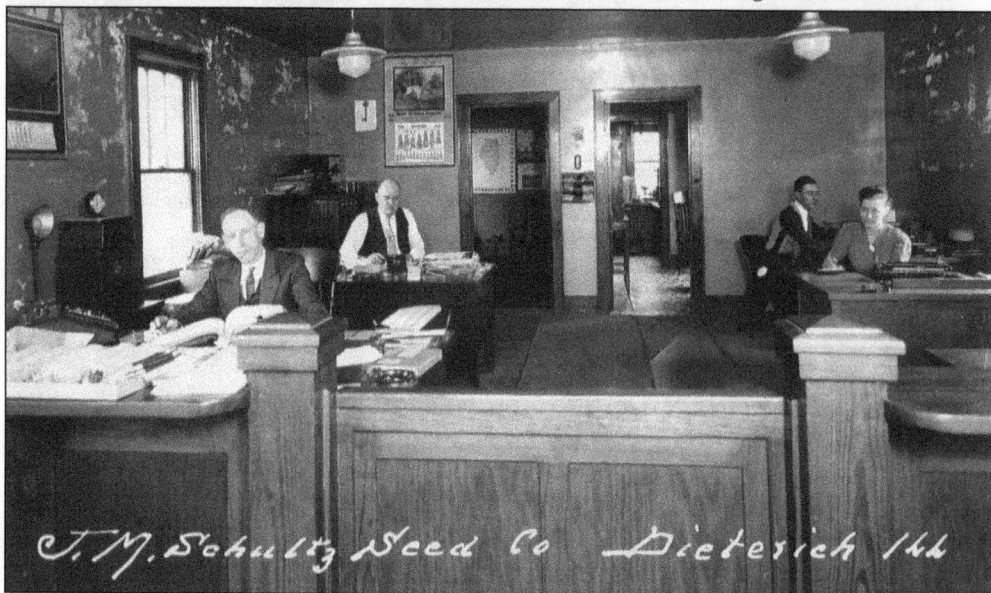

John M. Schultz was a young man of ambition in the early years of the 20th century. By the time this photograph was taken in 1939 at the company's Dieterich office, Schultz was one of the state's largest wholesalers of seed. Johnny B. Runde is on the far left, and John M. Schultz is next to him. Schultz's daughter Esther is on the far right and his son John H. is next to her. John H. Schultz conceived the cross at the crossroads and lived to see it completed in 2001.

Schultz Seed specialized in redtop and timothy seed, as the sign on the side of the building notes. Redtop and timothy are grass seeds that can be used for either hay or grazing. Both photographs were likely taken in the 1920s.

The Schultzes have always relied on trucks to move their product to the customer, as shown in these undated photographs.

Edgewood had a thriving business district in the early years of the 20th century. By the time this photograph was taken on February 16, 1908, the town had a downtown block of its own with, from left to right, a grocery, hardware, grocery, and meat market. As is the case in many small towns, much of those businesses have closed, although the town still has a grocery store.

"If those walls could talk. There's a lot of history in that house." That's what former resident Regina Baxter says about the old James Hotel on South Prairie Street in Montrose. The Baxters bought the old hotel in 1979 from the Blanche Bishop estate. Their son owns the home now. Railroad personnel utilized the home as a lodging facility in the days when railroad travel was more prevalent. This photograph was taken sometime before 1920, judging from the dresses worn by the women on the porch.

Like many small towns along the National Road, Montrose had its own railroad depot during the heyday of rail transportation. But like in many small towns, the trains no longer stop at Montrose, leaving little need for a depot, even one as stylish as this.

These young ladies braved the cold for an outing in southern Effingham County between Watson and Mason. Clockwise from the upper right are Ludie Keller, Beulah Martin, Verena Martin, Mayme Lamkin, and Josie Percival. Their friend Art Rice, a student at Illinois College of Photography, would take pictures of his friends on these outings. Rice later became a grocer in Watson. This particular picture was taken near the railroad bridge between Watson and Mason around 1914.

Kepley Springs is located just north of Mason. After Henry Kepley died in 1906, his widow Ada managed the farm of about 200 acres for several years. But the farm was also known as a gathering place for young people and families in the years on both sides of the turn of the 20th century, such as in this photograph.

Here is a group of ladies meeting at the Kepley Springs farm. One can see the sun peeking through the heavily wooded area.

The Kepleys were not the only people who enjoyed time in the country. Here are members of the Gravenhorst family and friends camping along the Little Wabash River south of Watson around 1920. The campsite was southeast of the old Oakview School, one of many rural schools that flourished in the county until the 1948 consolidation.

The Watson cannery factory provided employment for numerous people around the dawn of the 20th century. Shown are some of the employees who worked there. It was located directly east of the old flour mill and was owned by Bud Martin.

Shumway once had a thriving downtown. Laue Brothers, shown in the center of the photograph, was one of two hardware stores at one time. The building is now the home of Sutter Sanitation, which serves much of Effingham County.

Here is Watson as it looked in 1906, with IC tracks in the background. The town was founded around 1852 and was already a major shipping point for railroad ties and hoop poles by 1857. By 1890, the town had four churches, two hotels, four general stores, two sawmills, two blacksmith shops, two restaurants, a saloon, flour mill, drugstore, livery stable, canning factory, stove factory, buggy spoke factory, shoe cobbler shop, millinery shop, harness shop, and bottling plant. The town's commercial activity today is pretty much limited to a convenience store and grain elevator.

The Route 37 curve in Watson has always been a dangerous intersection. In this photograph, taken from the steps of Keller's Grocery in the late 1940s, this semitrailer has seen better days. One can see the sign leading to the old Texaco station in the center of the photograph. To its right is the old Ancient Free and Accepted Masons lodge. Keller's closed in the mid-1950s, and the building was torn down so that a new post office could be built.

Rice's store was a Watson mainstay for much of the mid-20th century. Opened in about 1928, Rice's sold just about everything. "You could hardly mention anything that wasn't in that store," said Melba Rice Henderson, the owner's daughter. Rice's array of merchandise is shown in this photograph. From left to right are employee Jake Rhode, Lora Henderson Rice, and W. A. (Art) Rice. The Rices sold the store to Woodrow Keller in 1946.

Art Rice bought his store building from Art Abraham, who had operated a similar store for many years.

This group at the T. H. Vaughn elevator sometime between 1938 and 1940 includes, from left to right, an unidentified salesman, owner T. H. Vaughn, and employees Reginald Flach and Carl Miller. Flach (1917–1997) invented a chicken feed mix that was a big hit throughout the area. He later worked at the old Norge plant in Effingham. Miller, who lived on the Montrose blacktop, went on to spend many years at Young Radiator in Mattoon.

At one time, the town of Mason had a public square. Since then, this little community in southern Effingham County has become like many small towns—a bedroom community for larger communities nearby, such as Effingham.

Mason was incorporated in 1865 and named for Roswell Mason, mayor of Chicago at the time of that city's great fire of 1871. Like many towns of that time, it was set up along a major railroad line—in this case the IC. Roswell Mason had superintended the railroad project, completed in 1856. By 1880, Mason had a population of 1,100. Here is the scene on January 25, 1912, when a devastating fire hit Mason.

Many Civil War soldiers returned to Illinois after their service. Here are some of them at the Mason Civil War Monument at the Mason Union Cemetery in 1909. Those identified are drummer Harry Thies, a Mr. Steele, Andrew Bailey, John Reid, A. J. Thomas, W. M. Reynolds, Peregrine White, David Schumacher, John Writer, Charley Wilson, and Elay Hardsock.

Eight

THE BROTHERS FITCH

Lewis Fitch (1844–1918), the middle of three Fitch brothers, sits in front of his jewelry shop at 205 West Jefferson Street in about 1900. He learned the jewelry trade from his father, Hiram, and moved to Effingham in 1879. After George Eastman invented mass photograph processing in the last years of the 19th century, Lewis became a Kodak dealer as well as a jeweler. His younger brother, Alfred, was better known as a photographer. In fact, Alfred took this photograph. Lewis died on November 6, 1918.

Alfred Fitch (1857–1905) worked as his brother's assistant, although he was best known as a photographer in his own right. It is believed that Lewis snapped this shot of his younger brother in 1893, right around the time that Lewis became a Kodak dealer. Neither brother married. In fact, their mother, Artemisia, moved to Effingham after the brothers did and died there in 1910.

From all accounts, Alfred loved capturing the spirit of his adopted hometown. Here is a shot of the railroad crossing guard at the IC tracks where they cross Fayette Avenue. The guard had a little shed to hang out in when he did not have to work. The city's old standpipe, or water tower, is shown in the background.

Train travelers and crews stopped for many years at Pacific House near the junction of the IC and Pennsylvania Railroads, as shown in this 1898 shot. The current Effingham depot is directly west of the Pacific House site.

Alfred Fitch, who was described in his obituary as an "exceedingly exemplary man," liked nothing better than to stroll the streets of his adopted hometown and snap photographs of his many friends. Here is Charles Miller and some pals in 1895 in front of the City Bakery and Confectionery, at 313 West Jefferson Street. The posters in front of the store are advertising something for Saturday, May 30.

Lewis Fitch got away from the store to take pictures too. Described in his obituary as "very emphatic in his likes and dislikes," Lewis wandered west of the IC tracks one day around 1900 to snap this photograph at Austin Lumber. Austin's trade in buggies would not last many more years. Lewis and Alfred owned the second automobile in Effingham, according to longtime *Effingham Daily News* correspondent Clem Thoele. It was a two-seater, one in front and one in back, with neither windshield nor top.

Street fairs were hugely popular around the beginning of the 20th century. Here is Alfred's shot of an arch advertising a street fair around harvest time.

African Americans have never been prevalent in Effingham, although the city is more diverse today than ever. This black workman, however, was in town in 1893 to work on the Austin Block on Jefferson Street between Fifth and Banker Streets. Here he is eating his lunch.

Here Alfred Fitch shows a panoramic view of the Austin Block construction site in 1893. The Mail Pouch sign would soon be obscured by the new building. No matter, the Blochs would soon commission barn advertising. Several Mail Pouch barns have been designated national historic landmarks.

Alfred Fitch enjoyed standing on the second stories of downtown buildings to pursue his hobby. Here he is shooting downward on a street fair around 1900. John B. Althoff is the horseman wearing a top hat. Note the drum major leading the band behind Althoff and his horse.

The Women's Christian Temperance Union was a major force in Effingham during the final years of the 19th century. Alarmed by increasing incidents of alcohol abuse, Effingham activist Ada Kepley crusaded against John Barleycorn for an extended period of time. In this photograph, Lewis Fitch is taking a photograph of photographers, including little brother Alfred, at left.

There is no evidence that Alfred had acrophobia. That is a good thing, because he did his share of climbing. Here he is in the courthouse clock tower looking north. St. Anthony Catholic Church is shown in the upper center of the shot.

Alfred got this shot of workmen digging a well on the northwest corner of the courthouse square at the corner of Fourth and Washington Streets. J. T. Waller ran a cash store across Washington at this time. While today's cash stores are short-term-loan businesses that charge exorbitant amounts of interest, cash stores of 100-plus years ago were simply general merchandise stores that traded goods for cash, as opposed to credit or barter.

Effingham County was first settled by folks coming down the National Road, 70-plus years before Alfred took this photograph in 1897. These travelers are climbing the hill into Effingham from the east on a dusty summer day.

119

Alfred Fitch walked into the Austin Opera House one day in the 1890s to shoot this photograph of a dramatic rehearsal. The opera house was the principal source of downtown entertainment before the advent of motion pictures.

Lewis and Alfred Fitch lived with their mother in this home alongside the IC tracks at 210 South Front Street.

Downtown denizens received a rude shock when brick on the southwest corner of the Effingham County Courthouse collapsed. Of course, Alfred Fitch was there with his trusty camera. The courthouse was repaired and stands today as a monument to times past.

It takes 10 minutes to get from Shumway to Effingham nowadays. When Alfred took this photograph around 1900, it took quite a bit more time by horse and buggy. This shot, facing east, shows the village's downtown to the left and what is now Plumb Park to the right.

122

Lewis Fitch was not above taking a break from his jewelry business. Here he sits on the step in front of the jewelry store at 205 West Jefferson Street.

Alfred Fitch liked to get out of town from time to time. This shot was taken at the old Effingham County Agricultural Fair.

A little girl is walking along an Effingham street in this 1898 shot. One can tell her approximate age by the fact that her dress is relatively short. As she got older, the dresses got longer.

Downtown Effingham was anchored by the Austin Block, completed in 1893. Here is an 1892 shot by Alfred of the construction process as it looked in the summer of 1892. The *Effingham Democrat*, directly north of the block, was one of four newspapers that merged in 1946 to become the *Effingham Daily News*. The current home of the *Effingham Daily News* is in the top center of the photograph.

The Fitch brothers, Lewis and Alfred, enjoyed experimenting in the darkroom, as evidenced by this double negative. These "two men" are actually the same man. Alfred took the same man posed differently in separate shots in 1893 and then combined the negatives in the darkroom.

Here a group is picnicking, probably at the fairgrounds, in 1899.

Visit us at
arcadiapublishing.com